Owl Coloring Book For Adults

An Adult Coloring Book Of 40 Owls in a Range of Styles and Ornate Patterns

Adult Coloring World

ISBN-13: 978-1519696670

ISBN-10: 1519696671

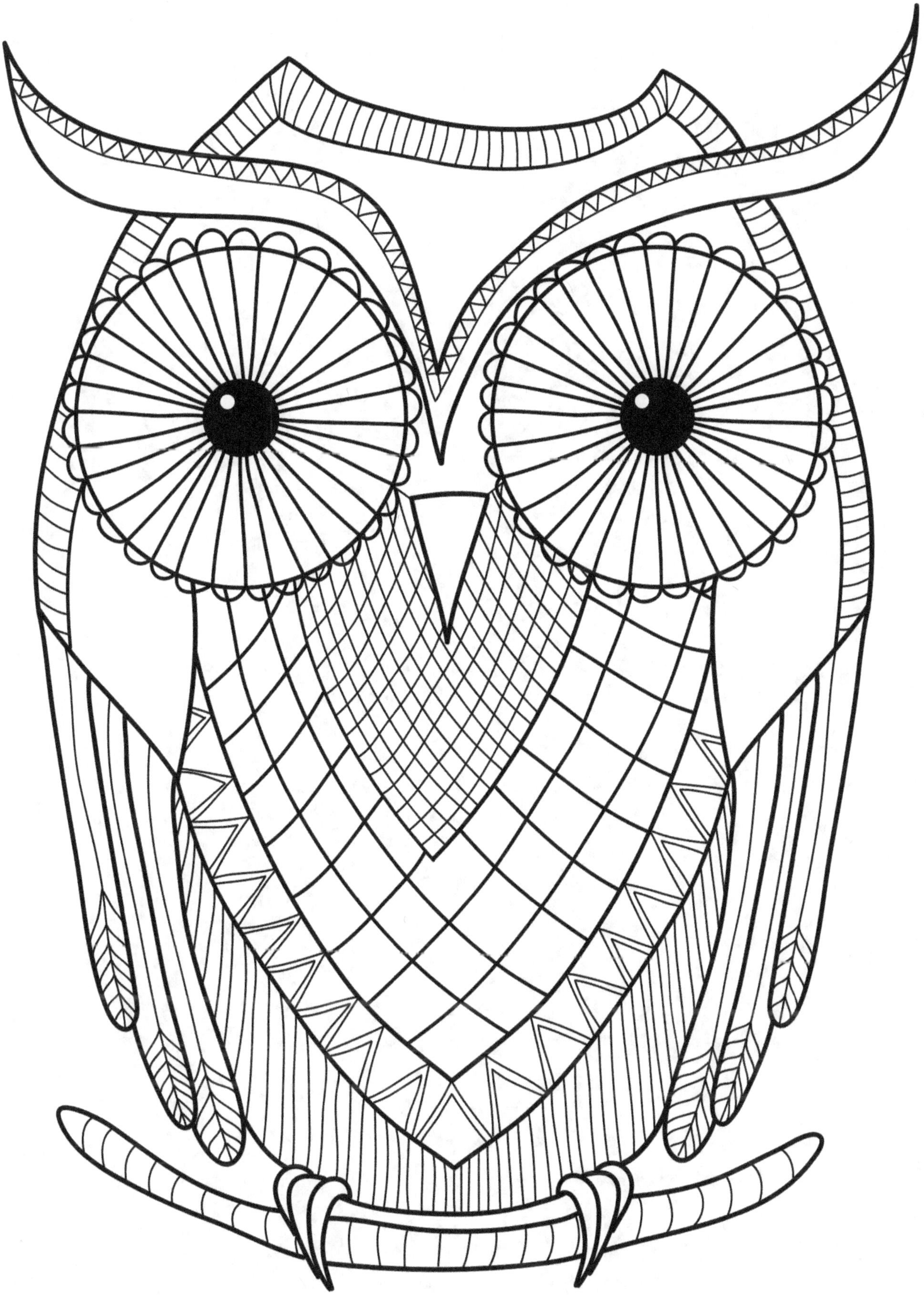

www.ingramcontent.com/pod-product-compliance
Lightning Source LLC
Chambersburg PA
CBHW081235280526
45787CB00006B/2672
* 9 7 8 1 5 1 9 6 9 6 6 7 0 *